The Big Six Get an Email

Published in the UK by
Scholastic Education, 2024
Scholastic Distribution Centre, Bosworth Avenue,
Tournament Fields, Warwick, CV34 6UQ
Scholastic Ireland, 89E Lagan Road, Dublin
Industrial Estate, Glasnevin, Dublin, D11 HP5F

1 2 3 4 5 6 7 8 9 4 5 6 7 8 9 0 1 2 3

Printed by Ashford Colour Press

The book is made of materials from well-managed,
FSC®-certified forests and other controlled sources.

	MIX
FSC	Paper from responsible sources
www.fsc.org	**FSC® C011748**

A CIP catalogue record for this book is available
from the British Library.

ISBN 978-0702-32732-2

Author
Jonny Walker

Editorial team
Rachel Morgan, Vicki Yates, Suzy Ditchburn,
Jennie Clifford

Design team
Dipa Mistry, Andrea Lewis and We Are Grace

Photographs
p4 (background) Verbena/Shutterstock
p8 (background) Omeris/Shutterstock

Illustrations
Martin Bustamante/Advocate Art Ltd

How to use this book

This book practises these letters and letter sounds:

or (as in 'worst')	oul (as in 'could')	are (as in 'dare')
au (as in 'taunt')	oor (as in 'poor')	tch (as in 'watch')
a (as in 'last')	a (as in 'salt')	st (as in 'castle')
ch (as in 'school')		

Here are some of the words in the book that use the sounds above:

worst   squad   prepare   applaud   match   talk

This book uses these common tricky words:

the   says   they   of   who   to   today

About the series

This is the third book in a fiction series about a group of monsters called 'the Big Six'. In the first book, the Big Six get jobs in a shop. In the second book, they go to an art gallery.

Before reading

- Read the title and look at the cover. Discuss what the book might be about.
- Talk about the characters on page 4 and read their names.
- The story is split into chapters shown by numbers at the top of the page.

During reading

- If necessary, sound out and then blend the sounds to read the word: sh-oul-d, should.
- Pause every so often to talk about the story.

After reading

- Talk about what has been read.

Big Six

Bob Socks

Goth

Chuck

Kit

Wet Hat

Ness

1

"It's the World Wide Web," Chuck declares. Bob Socks gasps.
"Could we watch cat videos?" Ness asks.

"We could!" says Chuck.
They all watch videos of cats getting
scared of cucumbers.

The computer bleeps.
"An email!" screams Goth. "I'll read it!"
They listen carefully.

Dear Worst Squad,

Let's see who the **true** Big Six is. Come to Salt Castle School at midnight.

The Better Big Six

"Rivals! How dare they?" Wet Hat shouts.
Kit flexes her muscles.

"Why should we fight them?" Chuck asks.
"Poor, scared Chuck," Bob Socks taunts.

"Listen, it's fine for you. They'll all target me, I'm a goblin. You're...laundry!"

"Pause this squabble!" Wet Hat interrupts.

"Prepare for battle, squad," commands
Wet Hat. "We should cause chaos.
We're monsters, after all!"

Chuck just glares while they applaud.

"OK, *fine*, Wet Hat," Chuck says.

"I'm going to be my true self today!" announces Wet Hat, pulling off his hat. "I will fight as King Lentil!"

"Let's go to Salt Castle School and defeat them," King Lentil thunders.

Chuck finds a handwritten note on the door.

The Big Six stare in shock.

Ness and Wormthing have a wrestling match. Ness squashes Wormthing until Wormthing submits.

00   01

Krak and Bob Socks have a swimming race.
Bob Socks absorbs the water. Krak wins.

Goth and Gums have an eating contest. Gums wins after poor Goth remembers she has no stomach!

02   01

Kit and Helmet play 'Stay Still'.
They freeze completely. Nobody wins.

King Lentil and Waspcat have a debate.
King Lentil wins with his impressive lecture.
Waspcat cannot talk.

The last match is a spelling contest between Chuck and Bugbear.

Chuck makes no mistakes. Poor Bugbear cannot even hold a pencil!

"We win!" the Big Six declare.
After the drama, the best monsters celebrate.